BLACK

THRIVING, SURVIVING

GIRL

AND "NO, YOU CAN'T TOUCH MY HAIR"

WHITE

AN ANTHOLOGY

SCHOOL

EDITED BY

OLIVIA V.G. CLARKE

BLACK GIRL, WHITE SCHOOL

THRIVING, SURVIVING AND 'NO YOU CAN'T TOUCH MY HAIR'

Edited by

OLIVIA V.G. CLARKE

LIFESLICE MEDIA

This book is dedicated to my family and friends who have supported me and loved me throughout my life.

To Mom and Dad: Thank you so much for the love and support you have given me. I couldn't be more grateful for everything you have done for me. You have provided me with so many incredible opportunities and the tools to grow. I'll forever be grateful to you. I love you guys so much.

To Gabrielle and David: I love you and can't wait to watch you grow up and flourish. I know I am leaving for college soon, but don't worry - I'll always be here for you.

This is also dedicated to Buckeye - I miss you buddy. I can't wait to see you again.

And most importantly this is dedicated to my Granny. I wish you had been able to see me graduate and become an author. I miss you every day. I love you.

PREFACE

Hello!

Welcome to Black Girl, White School. To whoever is reading this book - thank you for picking it up!

This book is a collection of poems, stories and anecdotes. Everything found between these pages was written by Black girls and women who are current or former students in predominantly white institutions FOR Black girls who have and are experiencing the same.

Students, parents, teachers, administrators or just casually curious readers - please pay close attention as you take a look into the minds of some amazing, powerful, and inspirational Black girls.

INTRODUCTION

This kind of crisis was not supposed to happen to kids like me. Not kids who had roots and training like I did. But it did happen.

Mom and Dad were in their late 20's and had been married for more than three years when they had me, the first of their three children. GenXers by age and spirit, Mom and Dad had both been Black activists and leaders, in various ways, going all the way back to high school and college.

They met in college, where Mom was a Journalism major and Dad majored in Black Studies and Political Science. They ran their own company together from home, so I was always with them when I wasn't in school. They surrounded me, my sister and brother with positive Black images, and influencers. I attended a primarily Black school. I am a member of a primarily Black church. At home, I'm surrounded by Black literature and art and my parents are always engaged in political and social discussions. They are known for their socio-political commentaries.

Their goal has been to raise their kids to be confident, prepared and productive people. To be proud to be Black. They knew my sister, brother and I would live as leaders and we would need to know and love ourselves. We were raised to appreciate all cultures and to cultivate and cherish good relationships with all people, but to never lose sight of our Blackness. To never stop fighting for equality, empowerment and the end of racist systems and ideology.

My mom and Dad are both inner city kids, who grew up in poor Black neighborhoods. Their parents struggled to send them to be educated in primarily white private schools in the 80's and 90's so they understood and prepared me for the mental and emotional impact the environment of an affluent PWI could have on me. At least... I thought I was prepared.

My mom is a powerhouse who stretches herself and sacrifices herself for us. She double and triple schedules herself, personally and professionally, to be able to, selflessly, still say yes to whoever needs her help outside of our home. (Dad says she, "burns her candle at both ends so others can have light").

She has actively sought out and secured opportunities and tirelessly advocated for me and my siblings, while being an active volunteer, caring friend, family member and dedicated consultant and writer. My mother's life and all of her resources have been dedicated to my and my siblings education and experiences.

She is everywhere. She never rests. She could have had material things. She chose to let go of personal comfort and place her emphasis on making sure that we have the strongest launching pad she can provide for us.

My dad approaches being a husband and father like it's an Olympic sport - with intensity and dedication (it's actually pretty comical at times). He's our advisor, coach, team builder and peacemaker. He's a fierce protector of our spiritual, mental and emotional selves, as well as our physical selves and a highly positive, patient, empathetic comforter.

He's a selfless provider who always puts himself last. He's a problem solver and judicious settler of disputes, but he's also the household's calm listening ear when any of us just needs to vent. In every way he can, he has placed his personal ambitions and comfort aside in order to make sure all of us can thrive in every way we can. He is dedicated to protecting our interests and our energy by giving us the support and latitude we need to do the more public things he can't right now. Mom and us kids are his world.

So training and exposure is not the problem. Parental guidance and involvement is not the problem. So, I was covered, right?

Nope.

I'm a year younger than my classmates. Ten, 11 and 12 year-old me was in for a shock and struggle that no one really knew about from 6th grade well into 8th grade. Discovering how to navigate a world that is often hostile toward you and learning how to walk with wisdom and confidence in the power of your Black womanhood is a process. High school freshman me emerged to become who senior me is now.

So many Black girls entering PWI's encounter a similar situation.

Despite their Black roots outside of school, they find themselves struggling in an environment that forces them to deal with the effects of systemic racism and prejudice in what should be a safe space.

After I became comfortable and secure in my Blackness again, I realized that I was not the only one. I decided to dedicate my time to helping other little Black girls feel seen and heard. I started with becoming active in diversity, equity, and inclusion work at school and gradually moved outward into the community. Eventually I started thinking about how I could create widespread change - that is how the idea for "Black Girl, White School" came to be. With the help of my incredible parents, I was able to make my dream come true. I was able to take the voices of amazing Black girls and women and present them to the world.

CONTENTS

THE THRIVE PLAYLIST

Hey check out this perfect playlist to vibe to while reading "Black Girl, White School."

SPOTIFY:
https://bit.ly/blackgirlwhiteschoolplaylist

APPLE MUSIC:
http://bit.ly/BlackGirlWhiteSchoolThrivePlaylistApple

ONE

CODE SWITCHING

CODE SWITCHING: THOUGH OFTEN SEEN AS PRIMARILY A linguistic phenomenon/adjustment, it is also known as when you tone down your Blackness to fit into a predominately white situation.

Every day I step into an institution where I often feel I cannot be 100% myself for fear that it will place me at a disadvantage... that I may lose social capital and respect. But as a Black girl, that is something I deal with everywhere: at school, at work, in public and in private. It is an extremely tiring experience.

As I walk through school, I see girls who are not Black wearing accessories or clothing created or popularized by Black people. I hear rap and R&B playing through their AirPods and I hear them using AAVE (African American Vernacular English) - oftentimes incorrectly - and yet...I have often felt the need to change *myself* when I get to school. I have felt the need to tone down my Blackness until it is palatable for others. That only the cool aspects of my culture is acceptable - while the struggle that goes hand in hand with my cultural reality is not welcome. That is, until it's time for a school cultural assembly or project.

So... when you see a Black girl in the hallway know that she may be performing two jobs at once: getting her education and attempting to fit in an environment that is dismissive or hostile to the woman she really is.

-OLIVIA V.G. CLARKE

HOW ASSIMILATION CHANGED MY IDENTIFICATION WITH MY CULTURE

BY TIARA MCKINNEY

In my last year of middle school, I found out that I would be attending a boarding school in New Jersey. My hard work, long hours spent studying, stress and anxiety would pay off - but I had no idea what to expect at my new school. I had never visited New Jersey before and the only communities that I knew were in my home country, The Bahamas.

I only knew my small island community where I went to school with many of my peers. I shopped at the same supermarket as most of them, and my parents and their parents worked together or knew each other. New Jersey is vastly different and I still have not fully adjusted. How do you ever fully cope with being away from home?

The first day of my freshman year came and I drove about five minutes from a borrowed apartment to the school at which I would be spending the rest of my high school years. My mother spoke calming words while I dragged suitcases and bins from our rented van to the room where I would live. The room was empty and bare with its menacing green carpets and cream-colored walls that reminded me nothing of home. I shrugged my way down the hallways of the red brick wall buildings to and from orientation meetings while other students strutted down the hallways as if they were runways. They were so sure of themselves... and they had whole family legacies at the school. I knew no one and I had no legacy. I felt out of place.

That first year, I rushed to learn everything about living in the United States and living closely with other people who looked nothing like me and who came from a variety of other backgrounds. I changed how I spoke and what I said. I felt it would be best if I didn't have an accent, so I tried to speak like the others around me. I unlearned how to be polite and how to greet people, how to smile to others and say good day. I learned how to just ignore people if we were in public. I unlearned my habit of calling my elders ma'ams or sirs. I did not realize that my learning of and adaptation to this new culture also came with the unlearning and erasure of the social customs and traditions that were representative of where I came from - of my culture and upbringing.

When breaks came I traveled home - but when I went home it felt different. I walked off of flights of cold, stale air into the fresh sea breeze that reminded me that I was home. I indulged in everything that I thought came with being a Bahamian: I went to the beach more often, I ate more pastries and food that I had previously taken for granted, and I visited family and friends whom I missed when I was gone.

However... I felt like a fraud.

I had learned everything about New Jersey culture and I could no longer appear authentic when I returned home. I was mocked for my Bahamian accent - or rather, my lack thereof. In all of the stores that I shopped at, family friends always thought it okay to stop me, my sister or my mother and ask what happened.

❝ "She sounds so 'American' now," they observed and at times, taunted.

It seemed, I could no longer be one of them.

I felt stuck in between two places, two people, and two cultures. To the students at my school, I was still not one of them and everything that I had tried to learn on the outside was a coverup for my background - about which I would never talk to them. To those in The Bahamas and more specifically my small island community, I could not relate to them either. I was a fake, someone who had not chosen to remember her roots and someone who had chosen to assimilate.

In my rush to learn what I thought I had to in order to fit in abroad, I risked feeling left out at home.

IS IT KAY?

BY KA'ISIS LEE

EVER SINCE ELEMENTARY SCHOOL, I'VE ALWAYS DREADED THE first day of school. Not because, "Oh no! new teachers!" - or - "Prepare for all nighter essays again..." No, I could handle that. I've always dreaded the first day of school simply because I knew that in every classroom I entered, the teacher inside would reach a certain point on the student list where the last names that begin with K and L met. I would know exactly when they got to that point because of their hesitation and the resulting dead silence in the room.

"I go by 'kay'" is what I learned to say. Now, I say it before they even try to pronounce it.

My real name is

K-A- apostrophe / ' - CAPITAL "i" NOT A "L" -S-I-S

KA'ISIS pronounced: KAY-ISIS

Think of how many teachers you've had in your lifetime. Even if you've only attended one school your whole life, you meet at least four new teachers every year. As someone with anxiety that becomes heightened in new environments, sitting through hundreds of sessions of teachers trying to figure out the best way to say my name feels ten times worse than it should. No, it doesn't help that I have social anxiety... no it doesn't help that I'm a person of color... and it definitely doesn't help that I have a naturally quiet voice.

So... whenever I tried to correct a teacher, the two possible outcomes of verbalizing this correction would, without exception, be:

Me: It's pronounced "kay-isis"

Teacher: kayesis?

Me: ...yeah.

-OR-

Me: it's pronounced "kay-isis"

Teacher: you need to speak up I can't hear you

Then, I'd be too scared to continue trying - so I'd just let it go.

IT'S NOT that I necessarily *wanted* to give up in those situations, but the awkward and embarrassing interactions were so intense and stressful for me that I would rather just drop the subject than to continue in that state of anxiety. I mean, it *is* calling for attendance after all. When the teacher calls your name, all the attention is on **you** - and I **did not** want to further extend the amount of time all of the focus was on me.

This is why the first day is agony for me. I know, at the beginning of the day, that when I walk into these new classrooms all I'll remember is the way the teachers said, "kalysis?... kahsis?... kaysis?" -

As if they're asking a question?

Making me feel like my name is a question?

Making me feel like my existence is questionable?

If you have a question about how to pronounce my name, the question *should* sound something like this - **"How do I pronounce this?"**

Over the years, I simply got tired of it. Tired of the disrespect. Tired of the disregard. Tired of the lack of effort. Tired of the lack of empathy.

I remember when a teacher did not feel the need to try and learn my name. Instead, she gave me the nickname "kay" - because kaisis was just too hard for her. She never asked if that was okay with **me,** but whatever makes them feel better, right?

So I started going by "kay."

It was a lot easier and less stressful to tell someone you go by "kay" than it was to try to get them to pronounce Ka'Isis correctly. I never really chose this name for myself - but I guess it's mine now.

I liked it for a while when my friends called me "kay," because it's like a cute little nickname and I don't know what other nickname you'd get from Ka'Isis. Definitely not "Isis" - I've been bullied enough about that one. But when teachers and adults call me that, it reminds me that I'm not Ka'Isis. For a period of time, I would even forget that Ka'Isis was my real name - until we had a substitute teacher.

Ka'Isis, to me seems, to be gone.

"kay" bends and twists herself into whatever other people want and over the years I've learned people like "kay" more than Ka'Isis... and maybe that includes me too.

IT'S IMPORTANT TO KNOW THE DIFFERENCE

BY GABBY ANTHONY

I HAVE ATTENDED PREDOMINANTLY WHITE SCHOOLS FOR NEARLY twelve years. Each year, I have progressively come to understand and distinguish the differences between three related terms: assimilation, code switching, and "acting white." Although these terms are synonymous and are often used interchangeably, they are completely different concepts.

Based on my experiences, forfeiting important aspects, or in extreme cases, every aspect of one's own culture to gain and maintain the approval of the dominant culture is assimilation. Assimilation is rarely a choice - minority groups, by various means, are usually forced to assimilate into a dominant culture. Showcasing what is often seen, subjectively, as socially acceptable traits and skills above other, often less valued (again, subjectively and according to where you are and who you are with) personality traits is code switching. Lastly, "acting white" is used to denounce the importance or accomplishments of an individual by referring to their success as "white."

Oftentimes, peers outside of my school environment have told me that I am "acting white" because of the way I sound when speaking. People have assumed that I sound too intelligent to sound anything other than "white." However, one can be successful, smart, and speak standard American English dialect without being or "acting white." What it means to be Black cannot be reduced to what dialect I use when I speak.

From my experiences in predominantly white schools, I have also learned that code switching is a preventive tactic used to advance oneself within a social hierarchy, depending on situational circumstances. My early confusion between assimilation and code switching led me to believe, erroneously, that anytime I chose to code switch, I was voluntarily attempting to assimilate to white dominant culture.

When making statements relating to one's Blackness, it is important to choose our words carefully. Lack of care and attention to the language we use concerning various facets of the Black experience can cause confusion in young Black children. It can even perpetuate a misperception that saying someone is "acting white" is an appropriate and fair response to witnessing Black students speak in a standard American English dialect, earn a good grade on a test, or even develop close relationships with white people.

Plainly stated, knowing the meaning and the differences between these terms is so important because it can reduce assumptions that Black people might have about each other and the assumptions that we might have about ourselves. When we see a Black student who prefers to speak in African American Vernacular English (AAVE) in most environments but then chooses to speak in standard American English in educational settings, it is wholly unfair to assume the student is trying to "act white" or "sound white." For that individual, code switching may be a tactic they use in predominantly white spaces to combat negative racial stereotypes, manage teachers' impressions, or to be elected to leadership positions. In situations such as these, this student's decision to not to use AAVE should not be looked down upon as an attempt to assimilate or "act white." Instead, the individual could be maintaining their Black identity while also making an intentional decision about how to navigate predominantly white spaces. Because code switching is situational, in schools that demonstrate a firm commitment to inclusion, Black students may find code switching useless and unnecessary.

I WISH that I had known the difference between these three terms in my early years. By coming to understand the differences between these words, I have also come to encourage and reassure myself that my reasons for how I present myself in predominantly white spaces are far more complex than a simple desire to assimilate or "act white." If we all use these three terms (assimilation, code switching, and "acting white") more clearly, then we can dissolve misconceptions concerning many Black students' behaviors in predominantly white schools.

THRIVE TIP:

" Tap into your sources of power.

There is so much really heavy content everywhere we look – television, social media...even conversations with friends and family can stir up a lot of emotions.

It is critically important to seek out authors, podcasts, YouTube videos and other forms of media that speak life into you.
Who are the people or programs that leave you feeling hopeful and inspired?

Flood your mind with those messages and surround yourself with positive people. "

REBA PEOPLES, M.D.
BOARD CERTIFIED PSYCHIATRIST
LIFE-LONG EDUCATION IN PWI

TWO
ON BLACKNESS

Oreo: Black on the outside - White on the inside

Dear Black Girl,

Your Blackness is something only you can define.

Primarily white society, whether consciously or unconsciously, often associates whiteness with being articulate, well-behaved, beautiful, and appropriate. You may be told:

> *"You speak so well...for a Black girl"*
> *"You are so pretty...for a Black girl"*
> *"Wow you act so white! I'm blacker than you are!"*

But know this. Your Blackness is undeniable and you do not have to adhere to society's idea of what Blackness is.

-OLIVIA V.G. CLARKE

BLACK TO BASIC AND BACK

BY KATIE QUANDER

I've attended four different schools, two different churches and lived in four different neighborhoods in Houston and Northern Virginia. But all my life, practically everywhere I've been, I've spent my time always being surrounded by people who were different from me. I never really thought about it - unless someone brought attention to it.

I came home crying to my parents the day my pre-school best friend told me, "Your hair smells weird." But even after that experience, it never registered how much I looked different or stood out... until eighth grade.

At the beginning of that year, my best friend and I would stay up late texting, ranting and talking about life. I even became his personal relationship counselor.

At some point, he started acting differently with his friends, including me. It was subtle at first. He made a small joke...

"You are so basic because you watch basic shows like *The Office* or *Grey's Anatomy.*"

It seemed like an inside joke, two friends laughing with each other, so I started to embrace my "basic" nature. With my acceptance came more "jokes," but they changed from calling me basic to calling me white. During lunch, he would insinuate that I did certain things to act more white.

At our holiday concert for choir, I came wearing heels, which I will admit were a little too high. But I still strode into that room confident in myself, my outfit, and my hair. I was a woman who could take over the world; I loved riding that high. That was, until I saw him and he made fun of my jumpsuit, my shoes, my earrings... everything. To top it off, he mocked, "I figured you would show up with your white people hair."

That was it. He had crossed the line.

You can call me basic every day. You can continue to make me feel less of myself without me even noticing. But no one has the right to make fun of the thing that has torn me down since I was six years old. I may not have understood the difference between Black and white people, but I always knew my hair was different. It wasn't straight like all the other girls' hair, so I asked my mom to let me straighten it with chemicals. Even then, my hair was still stiff. In seventh grade, I discovered what I had searched for since six: extensions! I could have hair that flowed and moved, like my friends' hair. I got to be, what I thought to be, "normal."

So... when he had the audacity to mock my hair... he lost his best friend.

Finally, I was determined to teach him his wrongs. I even made a list:

1.) Do you think that I have to like or dislike certain things because I am Black?

2.) Do you realize saying a Black person is trying to be white is racist?

3.) Do you realize how hurtful your words are?

4.) Do you even care?

Until this whole situation came about, I had been a positive and confident girl - but jab by jab, he had chipped away at my self assurance. He broke me down so much, I didn't know how to get the words out to adequately describe my feelings.

After school was out, there was a pool party for everyone in eighth grade. Naturally, all the girls were self-conscious about wearing swimsuits in front of everyone. I was worried about my hair. With my extensions, I keep part of my hair out to cover them. But that means part of the hair frizzes when it gets wet - much like most Black people's - but the extensions get slick. My plan was to keep my hair dry, but I decided to enjoy myself instead. So I dunked my head in the water.

My ex-best friend and I had been growing closer again because the mocking had slowed.

Yet he managed to ruin his second chance.

"It looks like your hair is falling out," he said.

"Haha. Funny." I replied in a sarcastic voice, not knowing what to say. That's when I knew I was finished.

Later, I sat in bed replaying that moment. I thought of all the times I've been insecure about my hair; that's when I crumbled to the bathroom floor, with tears streaming down my face. I thought about all the times he had called me white and basic, and I thought to myself, "What if he's right? What if I do act like a white person? What if I unknowingly try and want to be white? What if I am ashamed of my Blackness and put down all Black people?"

I finally realized something. This wasn't about me losing pride in my race. It wasn't about me at all. This was him putting ideas into my head. There's nothing wrong with me. I wasn't trying to be white. I was being myself. So I decided to get off my ass and stick up for myself.

I wrote a text, calling him out on everything he had done to me. When you text a person while you are angry or sad (or both in my case), you put all the emotion into a little blue bubble. I explained everything.

A weight flew off my shoulders. I felt myself grow three inches without my heels at the concert. I took pride in my words. I had done it: I had the confidence to explain how I felt.

Slowly, we've become friends again, but I know not to get caught up in the friendship. I don't let him say anything negative about me because I don't need that extra doubt in myself.

From this relationship, not only did I gain confidence, but I also discovered and owned my racial identity. I was able to see that others thinking I am being "white" isn't me denying my race, it's me finding out who I am in America today. I am a proud young Black woman, growing up surrounded by people unlike me - but that will never change who I know I am.

THRIVE TIP:

66 Yesterday is gone
and tomorrow has yet to reveal itself.

Explore today with wonder
and excitement.

Live fully in each moment
of this day. 99

JOCELYN M. ARMSTRONG, ESQ.
12 YEARS PWI

THREE

I'M NOT HER...

DEAR ADMINISTRATORS, TEACHERS AND STUDENTS AT PWI's:
Learn your Black students' names.

We do not all look alike and we have our own names. When you fail to recognize that, you strip us of our identities. When you can remember the names of all of your white students, but mix up the few Black students you have - it is embarrassing and dehumanizing. There are only a few of us. You can take the time to learn our names.

If you can take the time to learn various other European names that are difficult to read and pronounce, then you can learn how to say Black students' and other students of color's names that also may be, initially, hard to read or pronounce. Don't give us a nickname if we do not tell you to. Do ask how to pronounce our names and make the effort to remember.

Equity and inclusion in education means you can take the time to learn our names.

- Olivia V.G. Clarke

SEE ME

BY COURTNEY PASCOL

I am not her.
Do not call me by her name, that is not me
we are so different, it's not hard to see.
Just because our color appears to be matched
does not mean our identities have to be attached.
Why can't people just take one extra second
To go beyond my outside and learn that we are not all
    the same?

I am not them.

Every Black person is not identical,
yet the blame placed on all of us for acts of violence is
    plentiful.
Our skin does not place us all in one box
We are not the same slaves that would harvest your
    crops.
Don't live in the past, please see what is true.

*Just because they look like me doesn't mean that's
    what I believe and do.*

I am me.

I am Black, strong and beautiful,

I am far from ordinary and usual.

I am a unique and intelligent woman

I deserve to be respected as a human.

Remember next time you see me anywhere

I am so much more than the color of my skin.

THRIVE TIP:

As Black women, our strength is legendary.

But remember, there is strength in vulnerability.

You deserve to be cherished.
You deserve care.
You deserve protection.

Never let anyone use your strength
as an excuse to deny your humanity.

As a free Black girl you have the right to be
wonderfully flawed,
emotionally dynamic
and fully you.

TERREECE M. CLARKE
CEO & AUTHOR
10 YEARS IN PWI

FOUR

BLACK GIRL MAGIC

You are the start of all life.
You are the beginning of civilizations and cultures.
You are Mother Nature and the Sun, personified.
You are magical.

-Olivia V.G. Clarke

CROWNS UPON MY HEAD

BY AMINAH ALIU

I WAS BORN WITH TWO CROWNS
    Each one as dark as I am
    Each one with a heritage so robust
    That it could part the Red Sea

I WAS BORN with two crowns
    One is thick, curly and long
    It grows towards the sky as grapevines do
    The other is a sacred diadem
    Fashioned from cloth and safety pins

I WAS BORN with two crowns
    And in the hours when the sun retired below the horizon
    I would practice wearing my crowns
    Climbing onto the bathroom counter
    I'd stare at my type 4 curls
    Trying to memorize their natural bends, angles, and frayed ends

Standing before my full-length mirror
I'd pin my hijab into place, perfectly
No piece of fabric was out of place

I WAS BORN with two crowns
And though I find it hard not to be angry at a society
That see two curses – not two crowns – upon my head
My mother always reminds me:
Sweetest daughter of mine–
Own your melanin
Own your heritage
Raise your chin
Do not let your crowns fall
When the sun is in its golden hour
Your melanin is fine like honey
And you are beautiful

DEAR BLACK GIRL

BY TIIA MCKINNEY

Dear Black girl, own your melanin
Be proud of the skin you're in
Raise your head, take a picture
When the sun is bright and shining
Your melanin is honey
Your skin glows, it is blinding

The smell of sweet coconut when you
Shake your curls
The boldness of your step
That is the power of Black girls
Raise your head once more
You are beautiful, be sure

Be sure of your beauty
A powerful Black girl's beauty

FALLING IN LOVE WITH BLACKNESS: THE MAGIC OF A COLLECTIVE

BY TIIA MCKINNEY

WHEN I WAS A LITTLE GIRL I ALWAYS LOVED TO GET MY HAIR straightened. I remember my stomach jumping in anticipation for my flowy, black locks to finally be silky and flowing down my back. My twin sister and I would stand in our small bathtub overlooking the brown lawn as we fought over who would be first to go to the front of the tub near the faucet to get her hair washed.

My mother would stand outside the tub and turn on the water, getting those clear plastic bottles of shampoo full of colorful sludge and artificial fruits. Then, one after the other, she would wash our hair and when we were all done, she would get the towels from down the hall in our linen closet and wrap our hair up to dry in a way that only she could. Next, she would take us to our room and bring a kitchen chair near the mirrored dresser. On it, she would have heat protectant spray and a hot pink flat iron that, with its high temperature, would lay down my unruly kinks.

My sister and I would each want to be the first one to get our hair straightened. My mother would start at the back of our necks with our curly, thick roots clumped up together like balls of tangled fur and she would go over it until our hair was straight and laying flat down our backs.

I never understood what was so special about my natural hair. I didn't understand why God had given me and my sister curly, kinky hair instead of the straight hair that was plastered on every tv screen. I couldn't understand why my hair couldn't be long without a flat iron or why my hair always had to be plaited up instead of loose, free and reaching out to the sun. I never understood the power of my melanin, but now I understand that Black is magic. I understand that I stand out and that I am both a part of a group and an individual within my culture. From my red undertones, to my shimmer in the sun, to my kinky curls, I am unique.

When I bought my first jar of leave-in conditioner and when I stood in my tub at school combing through my curls, I understood that Black was beauty. Nowadays, I don't care if my Afro is tangled in a bun, standing upright in a pineapple, down and flowing, or combed out to the sky, because I know that my Afro is a part of me.

I know that my skin is a beautiful part of me, too. My skin is beautiful. Whether in the dim of my room or in the light of a new day under the clear sky, my skin is beautiful. I don't care about the jokes people tell about not being able to see Black people in the dark, because I know you can see the truth in my eyes and the shine of my teeth. I know that even in the dark, you can see that I fill up the room, that I am a Black woman, that I occupy space, and that I am meant to be here. That is Black Girl Magic.

Black Girl Magic is not just the mirror pictures and the golden hour selfies, but rather, the group pictures that remind me that Black Girl Magic is about a collective team. Black Girl Magic means that we are powerful beyond measure, that we Black girls are done being silenced for our skin or for our gender.

Even though Malcom X said, "The most disrespected person in America is a Black woman," we Black women show up and recognize our position and our abilities. Even if we have to force America to listen to us, our Black Girl Magic and our collective strength will get us through and we will be heard. Black Girl Magic reminds me that I am unique, but that I am also an individual part of a whole - part of a collective. Black Girl Magic means that even if I don't feel strong enough, there are Black girls who will stand up on my behalf and stand for us all. We also stand up to fight for our Black fathers, brothers and friends. We consistently take on leading roles and responsibilities on the front lines in the fight against injustice.

So, I don't care how long my hair takes to style. I don't care about the way white girls are portrayed as superior in the media. I don't care if I'm told that as a Black woman I have no say, that I am too loud or too much. My Black Girl Magic makes me stand up. My Black Girl Magic helps me to believe in myself, to be a leader - to be a movement.

Black. Black. Black.

I am Black.

I am Black Girl Magic.

We are Black Girl Magic.

MIRROR MIRROR ON THE WALL

BY NDEYE THIOUBOU

Mirror mirror on the wall
I must admit
I love what I see
Reflected there
A girl, she seems happy
I mean, she's smiling after all
Her white teeth blind
The teeth stand out against
Deep brown chocolate skin
She got that from her father
Her mother is more caramel
Shades of Brown
Shades of Africa
Shades of Senegal
Stunning nonetheless
Her hair is special
It defies gravity
With no work
The tightly coiled

Kinky dark brown hair
Points up towards the sky
The sun
The moon and the stars
Mirror mirror on the wall
I hope that girl knows
She is
Beautiful

REPEAT

BY GABRIELLE CLARKE

She's extraordinary
:)
Smile
Wake up
Smile
Listen
Smile
Clean
Smile
Cook
Smile
Sleep
Smile
Repeat
Don't say anything
Smile more
Be seen
Smile more
Not heard

Smile more

Sit down

Smile

Chin up

Smile

Stay proper

You can't have more than me

Stay quiet

You can't do what I do

Stay quiet

You're inferior

Stay quiet

Weak

Stay quiet

Don't trip

Don't

/F

/A

/L

/L

Stay Quiet

no no

no no

no no no no

no no no no no

no nono no no

{Ruth Bader Ginsberg}

Luck

{Mae Jemison}

Coincidence

Be quiet
Put up with it
Try harder
Over and
Over
And **over**
And **over**
How do you do it?
Society, stop **screaming**
I'll **speak up**
I'm **not weak**
Maybe I'll
/F
/A
/L
/L
But I'll get up
And **I beat you**
In **every** way
With
A
Smile
She's extraordinary

THRIVE TIP:

Your voice matters.
You will have people throughout your life
that will try to convince you that it doesn't,
and that could cause you to get quiet.

Don't shut up for anyone!

Use your voice, keep talking, speak up.
And if they still refuse to hear you,
remember that your voice still matters,
and listen to yourself.

COMFORT WITCHER
PHOTOGRAPHER
16 YEARS IN PWI

FIVE

MINORITIES UNITE

Dear fellow minority students, faculty, parents, and staff,

WASSUUUUUUP! *fist bump* It's rough out here.

No, but seriously, hey. Just like being a Black girl at a PWI has its challenges, being a non-Black POC also brings its own struggles. We may not always face the exact same problems, but we can relate to each other. Being one of the only *insert racial minority here* kids at school is really hard. Suddenly and often unfairly you become a representative for all people of your ethnic background. I mean how are you supposed to speak for your *entire* culture, especially knowing your culture is not monolithic?

I used to think I was alone, but I came to realize that one of the best ways to get through the trauma was by talking to other kids going through similar situations. Being able to talk to other POC students and staff about my problems is one of the things that helped me get through rough times. Unfortunately, POC kids don't really get to see themselves represented at PWI's. So, when they do find faculty that share similar experiences it is truly a joy and a relief!

Remember that as minorities we face endless challenges and as a result, are incredibly strong. Stick together and fight for change. We are stronger together than we are apart.

- OLIVIA V. G. Clarke

P.S. I WANT to give a special thank you to the teachers of color who have provided me with support and guidance throughout the years. Thank you for being there for me in an environment where no one else understood. You have impacted my life more than you will ever know.

SISTER AFRICANA

BY SARAH HOLSTON

My doctor is a group of girls, shoulders touching
    around a small room, the sounds of our joy never
    stretching beyond its walls.
Every week we tackle spring cleaning: opening the
    wounds left by others and patching them up with
    something stronger to carry us through.
The smiles made here are of a different caliber--
More vibrant, maybe, more wide, maybe, more me
    than I had ever let myself feel before.
Because our happiness is a threat outside the room,
    our anger is turned into poison, our sadness is a
    wayward sword to be carefully ignored.
Early I learned to forget, the emotions I keep tucked
    away like snow shovels in the summer,
Were not meant for harsh eyes and invasive whispers.
My anatomy was not made to feel so unbeautiful and
    yet my eyes can't erase the ugliness they've been
    taught to see.
So, my doctor heals. And laughs. And leads.

And combs every knot, twist, and bunch out of my
  Afro--maybe out of my life.
I can pass around drops of honey and melanin to
  sip on,
Because medicine is what we call sisters and recovery
  is called family.

THRIVE TIP:

If you feel you are being gaslighted...
If you feel it is being insinuated that you do not deserve to occupy the space you are in...
If you feel that you are constantly having to prove your worthiness to have a seat at the table...

Guess what?
Your feelings are correct.

What should you do?
Stop, drop and roll.

Put the fire out in your mind, body and spirit.
Guard your heart by thinking on all the reasons you have earned your place.
Know that you deserve to be in that space and understand that your seat at the table is just as important as the others around you.

You are not an imposter.
Walk away when you get ready or make them put you out.

JOSLYN JONES
MECHANICAL ENGINEER
13 YEARS IN PWI

SIX
WHAT I WISH I HAD

Looking back on my years at a PWI, I have experienced more than a few micro-aggressions or instances of discrimination. I often wish I had someone there with me who would've told me what to do in those instances. I wish *I* could go back in time and help *me*.

I had a lot of insecurities in middle school, one being my hair. One day at school, I was wearing my hair in a big poof and I remember people comparing my head to broccoli. I remember everyone at my lunch table laughing at me while holding up broccoli to my head to emulate my hair. I remember girls who I didn't even really talk to coming from their table to take pictures and laugh along. At some point someone picked up a burnt one to say that this one looked more like me.

Honestly, the memory is a little blurry. I tried to forget it. I remember getting really upset and being on the verge of tears, so I left lunch. Later on I was told I was being too dramatic and it wasn't that big of a deal. To be honest, I self-deprecate a lot and I can't remember if I started this joke by accident or not. I wish I could remember it better, but I felt so awful...I just blocked it out.

Whether I started the joke by criticizing myself or not - that didn't give other people the right to rag on me. And that took me a while to realize. Humor is a common coping method. A joke made between two Black people doesn't invite non-Black input. A self-deprecating joke does not invite others to make the same joke about you. I might've compared myself to a burnt piece of broccoli - but that wasn't permission for everyone else to do the same.

When you experience something like this - or something that just doesn't sit right with you - talk to someone. A trusted teacher, a Black upperclassman, anyone who you feel comfortable with. It'll be okay.

I wish I had another Black woman at school to talk to. I wish I had felt confident enough to bring it up.

- OLIVIA V. G. Clarke

YOU BELONG

BY MARISSA GLONEK

To a Younger Me Attending PWI's,

You belong.

Some will ask why your hair is not straight like theirs.

Your curly crown will be healthy and resilient despite applying chemicals to fit in.

Some will ask if you were adopted because your mother is white. You will be proud of both your African and Polish heritage.

Some will stare at you in history class to gauge your reaction to slavery. Your ancestors were innovative, strong and led the way for you.

Some will use the "N-word" as a joke to see if you feel anything hearing it. You cannot have growth and change without feeling uncomfortable.

Some will listen to your music and use your lingo, but not come over for dinner.

You will find your tribe later in life and they will appreciate YOU in addition to your skin tone.

Some will assume you cannot be smart and share the same experiences as the next Black girl. You will uniquely own your experiences and share them in your Masters' classes.

Some will tell you the lighter your skin, the more beautiful you are.

You will learn to celebrate all hues of brown and black. It is the skin of kings and queens. You will think you do not belong. But, then....

You will take classes on Black excellence in college because it was not taught in elementary, middle or high school.

You will join Black organizations, a Black sorority and be tapped into a Black woman's honorary to uplift your community.

You will use your power in your career and personal life, while still finding your way. You are a voice for the next Black girl at a PWI who thinks she doesn't belong.

YOU BELONG.
Love, Me

WHO I WAS VS WHO I BECAME

BY MCKENZIE STRINGER

AT TEN YEARS OLD, WALKING INTO MY NEW MIDDLE SCHOOL with no friends and no expectations of what the next three years would be like left me slightly terrified. Not only was I so young, but I was so different from everyone I had seen since the moment I walked into the building. Blonde and brunette haired girls with high voices were running through the halls asking their friends how their summers went - but no one came up to me. Instead, almost silent whispers of "who is she?," was all I heard. After a few weeks of not knowing where I fit in and questioning whether this was the place for me, I had a decision to make... how would I fit in?

Over time I began to change myself - making adjustments to the old me to create a new me that I felt would be acceptable in my new environment. All I could think about was how people would react to my new hair and slightly higher voice. Would they finally accept me into their group or would they continue to treat me like I was invisible? I began to heavily consider the opinions of my "friends" before I made any decisions for myself. "Will they still like me if I do this?" Not only were my thoughts consumed with anxiety about everyone else's feelings and opinions, but my hair was no longer mine. The constant straightening of my hair eventually took a toll on my curl pattern. Instead of the curls I had when I first walked into school, there were now straight pieces in the front of my hair. I was so devastated, I cried - wondering why I had ruined something that made me, me. Experiencing this immediately made me question if what I was doing was right. Was changing myself and acting like someone I wasn't, just to fit into a specific friend group, the right thing to do?

After years of going through this endless cycle of continuously looking for the approval of others regarding outfits, boys, and even Instagram pictures, I had enough. I began to rethink all of the choices I had made to please everyone else.

I couldn't remember the last time I did something I enjoyed simply because I enjoyed it. I knew I had a problem when my mother couldn't even recognize who I had become. I could no longer live for someone else. Going into high school, I knew that something had to change. This was when I decided to ask myself a few questions.

"IS THIS REALLY WHO I AM?"

"Does the texture of my hair really define me as a person?"

"Are these people really my friends if I have to change myself for them to accept me?"

Walking into the entrance doors with my head held high and a smile on my face, I felt like a different person. My eyes were brighter, my heart was lighter and my spirit was freer. Through self-reflection and spending time with family and the people who have always supported me, I found who I was. No longer was I the girl who was a follower. No longer was I the girl that depended on others' approval to make decisions. I was the girl who didn't care if someone didn't like what I was wearing, or how my hair looked. I wasn't looking for approval from anyone. As long as I was happy, that was all that mattered.

DEAR ME

OLIVIA V. G. CLARKE

Dear Olivia,

Congratulations on making it to Middle School! I know how excited you are to go to your new school. I'm proud of you. You've worked so hard. You are about to step into a space with girls who hold a very different experience from your own. Most are privileged in ways that you will never be. Do not be discouraged. Know that you are enough and so much more. I wish I could stop you but I know that you will wish that you were white. You won't say it but you'll express that thought through your desires. You will say:

"I wish my hair was straight."
"I wish my skin was lighter."
"I wish I was mixed with something."

But hear me when I say that you are beautiful. Your culture is something to be proud of. Yes you are different, but I'll let you in on a secret... you are jealous of the white girls in your school. But guess what?

The music they listen to, the clothes they wear and the culture they enjoy... That's all Black culture baby! That's you. Be yourself. Take pride in what you have. Take pride in your gorgeous hair and your beautiful melanin. You are enough. You're beautiful ... I know no one tells you that at school. The boys at dances ignore you and you're constantly trying to look like the popular white girls.

But girl - I am begging you - put that flat iron down. Heat damage is real. It will take a while, but remember to love yourself. I'm working on it too. I love you.

Sincerely,
Olivia
P.S. I'm a senior now...don't grow up too fast

THRIVE TIP:

Often..
.Love on yourself
Laugh at yourself
Rest yourself
Forgive yourself...
Often...
Never let anyone take you laugh away!

THERESA A. BUSH

MARKETING COMMUNICATIONS MANAGER
5 YEARS IN PWI

SEVEN

RESILIENCE

1. *Know that you are enough. Don't fall victim to imposter syndrome.*

2. *Remember that you are beautiful. You're not ugly because you don't look like the girl everyone wants to be - she's white. Of course you don't look like her. Her beauty does not detract from your own. You're gorgeous.*

3. *Find a teacher who you can keep it real with. It will make school so much better.*

4. *When facing injustices remember there is strength in numbers. Band together and make a difference.*

5. *If the administration isn't listening - be organized and persistent. Remember, you can't always get everything you want, but you do deserve to be treated fairly. Your voice matters.*

6. It's okay to concede in a battle. You can't win every time. You deserve a break from fighting all the time. Focus on what is most important.

7. Become comfortable with saying no. It'll save you so many tears. Boundaries are healthy. Truthfulness is healthy. **No** is a healthy word.

8. I promise you there are people of all races who will date Black girls. Don't waste your time on the people who won't. You deserve better.

9. It's okay to call people out on their use of AAVE. No one wants to hear people walking around saying, "And that's on period no-cap pooh. Whew chile anyways lowkey."

10. It is not your job to educate others. They have Google. They have access to resources. If you feel up to it - go for it. But it's not your job.

-OLIVIA V. G. CLARKE

REMEMBER YOU ARE ENOUGH

BY YOLANDA DURDEN

WITHOUT EXCEPTION, I HAVE ALWAYS ATTENDED predominantly white schools. From kindergarten through high school, college and graduate school, I lived in a Black neighborhood, attended a Black Church, and was, obviously, part of a Black family. Being a Black female can sometimes be a challenge because in some environments you will be considered a double minority. My parents made sure I developed and maintained healthy relationships within each of my social circles, so I knew who I was, no matter who I was around.

When I was very young, my parents told me that I didn't have to be the best at anything - I just had to try my best in everything. They taught me to respect my friends and their cultures and reminded me, when my head got big with conceit, or when I felt like a failure, that I wasn't better than anyone - and no one was better than me. By holding on to these truths, I always knew, no matter what anyone said, if I put in the effort, I'd be satisfied with the outcome.

Life experience will teach you who really likes you for just being yourself. In most cases, your parents are your biggest cheerleaders and have your best interest at heart. As you grow into adulthood, be sure to seek several sources of wisdom and support to be there when times get tough. Find individuals who can make your hard days a little easier; people with whom you can celebrate your victories... people who can lend a listening ear in good and bad times. My family, friends, neighbors, coworkers, and church family remind me that I am always enough.

Know this... You are enough, too.

THRIVE TIP:

In life we are all guaranteed to have ups and downs. Sadly, some of the "downs" may make you doubt yourself, question your abilities or whether you belong.

Despite all the environmental factors that you may encounter in life remember to Never Give Up.

Stay strong and be unstoppable in pursuit of what sets your soul on fire.

In the end everything will turn out just right, the way God designed it to be.

The key to having unstoppable ambition:
*Be Persistent
*Be Determined
*Be Consistent
*Be Committed
*Be Diligent
*Be Tenacious
*Be sincere in everything that you do

SANDRA ALOT BROGDON
PUBLISHER, ROLE MODEL MAGAZINE
3 YEARS IN PWI

EIGHT

PERMISSION TO BE VULNERABLE

As a Black woman you are incredibly strong and powerful.

However, you don't have to be strong all of the time. It is not your job to be the rock. You need someone to lean on, too. It's okay to admit you need help or that you are overwhelmed. It is okay to be vulnerable.

Call a friend.

Write a letter.

You don't have to mail it anywhere.

The worst thing you can do is hold it all in. You don't have to be the magical negro who becomes a supporting cast member to everyone else.

-OLIVIA V. G. Clarke

MAKING AMENDS

BY AMINAH ALIU

Dear freshman Aminah,

I CAN HARDLY FIND your transparent reflection among the pillows, blankets, and loose apologies. I'm so sorry. It's a Thursday afternoon and you're sitting in math class, utterly confused. You're scared by the inadequacy this confusion breeds in you, but you're even more scared to ask for help, worried that your teacher will deem you unintelligent and proceed to ship you back to the public school you came from. To cope with this confusion, you zone out, counting how many white, Asian, and Black students there are in your class. You keep counting and recounting, but that doesn't change the fact that you are the only Black girl, the only Black person, in the room.

You're trying so hard to hold back your tears, but suddenly it's just too much and you're sitting in the nurse's office, crying. You're so tired – so nearly afraid – of what the future holds that your brain has left your body in search of other vessels. Your body has lulled itself to sleep on the sounds tears make when they're tired of falling. But, I should back up...

In the transition from a public middle school to the private, predominately white school you currently attend, you lost everything you once knew. You no longer existed among a majority of people who looked like you, and you were frightened to find that you could no longer rely on the automatic sense of belonging that gave you. The color of your skin was no longer something you could overlook. In the classrooms where you were the only Black girl—the only Black person—you felt betrayed by the school that let you in but didn't know how to keep you from falling apart.

As I think about these moments—and there were many of them—I realize the utter fallacy of mirrors and I now understand the definition of brokenness to be when the simple fact of your existence is an act of defiance against the ghost reflected back to you in the mirror. Indeed, you felt as though your new school had admitted your body, your skin, while leaving the rest of you behind.

But I know that you were aware of this great irony long before I was. You understood that the true price of a private school education was more than the marketed $36,000 per year; you understood that its broken System—the System that had broken you by making you feel that you were trivial—was the same one that patched you back up in the nurse's office that day, complete with a popsicle and a pat on the back. You understood this irony and blatantly refused to look at it. After crying yourself to sleep for two hours, you proceeded to splash your face with cold water, pack your bag, and head off to tennis practice as if this was all nothing but a bad dream.

I am writing this letter to you because I think that it may, in some way, help you move on. I believe that a refusal to look is no longer an acceptable way of protecting oneself from pain.

It has been three years since that afternoon in the nurse's office, and I still think about what happened. These musings have led me to one conclusion: maybe it is not so important to be broken or whole as it is to be mendable... healable. Is not our redeemability the definition of hope? Is it not the thing that brightens our futures and puts them back within reach? I am not here to say that you must fall in love with your wounds nor find a home within them, but rather that you must make enough peace with them to look at them candidly. You can not heal the brokenness that you will not look directly in the eye, and a ghost in the mirror is the surest sign that you have lost sight of what it means to be human. This past year, I can say that I've started to revisit the memories from that day and come to terms with the lessons I learned. I am able to understand that ninth grade was difficult not because I was a bad student, but because adjustment to a new normal is never easy.

You have always wanted the world to devote itself entirely to being either broken or whole, but I think if that was the case, then there would be no such thing as history, no sentimental, imperfect human narrative to look back on. I will not be the first to tell you, Aminah, that the world in many ways has always been broken, and you are not the first to experience this on a personal level, but I think that there is meaning in that brokenness, meaning that we can only find if we allow ourselves to be broken in this moment. We need to be able to look at our reflections in the mirror without hating the things that we see there.

Always remember this: when you sat there crying in the nurse's office, someone made enough peace with your brokenness to see the ways in which you were still whole. I'm sorry I didn't do that sooner, but now it's my turn.

WITH ALL MY LOVE,
        junior Aminah

NINE

AND...

THE WEIGHT OF A WHITE WORLD

BY SORAYA PATTERSON

Carrying just jokes and puns
Is a really sweet treat.
Carrying just witty remarks
Is quite an easy feat.

Carrying just derogatory words
Might cause you to sweat.
Carrying just a lower grade
Poses a little more threat.

Carrying just the fear of authority
Will get you off track.
Carrying just worry while exercising
Feels like a heart attack.

Carrying just a knee in your neck
Makes you feel 1000x older.
Carrying just a bullet in your body
Might just shatter your shoulders.

To experience all these things,
Or even just a few.
Is a task every day
That all Back people must do.

So we learn to take a hit
And how to get by
We learn to brush it off
Because it's all fine—

Right?

It's not always a group effort
Sometimes we're all alone
Carrying the weight of a white world
All on our own

DEAR YOUNGER ME

BY SORAYA PATTERSON

DEAR YOUNGER ME,

I know it's hard being the only Black kid in your grade. I hate to break it to you, but it's going to be like that until you reach middle school. I know it's hard being the center of the rude "jokes." I know it's hard being excluded from the big games on the playground. I know it's hard feeling like you don't fit in with anyone at your school.

I know you feel like your efforts go unnoticed - like when you clean up first but still get picked last to line up for recess. I know you feel disheartened when the rules change at the last minute - like when you make it to the line first, but it turns out you still didn't win since the other girl had "better form." I know that the only people you learn about in school have the same amount of melanin - with the exception of your Rosa Parks presentation in third grade. I know that you feel inferior to your teammates - especially when the coach only glances at one or two of your routines, but carefully and conspicuously watches several of everyone else's routines.

To avoid being thought of as ungrateful, spiteful, jealous, and angry, you stay quiet. To avoid being ostracized, bullied, neglected, and shunned, you try to change who you are.

I know that since you don't fully understand bias or racism, you subconsciously find a way to make sense of your predicament and come up with a conclusion that aligns with your feelings and observations:

In order to be noticed

In order to have friends

In order to be successful at any school activity

In order to be important enough to be remembered after you die,

You have to be white.

But I want to tell you:

You are a Black girl in a white school, and that is a fact. You will never be like the majority population of your school, so stop making that your goal. Microaggressions will follow you throughout your life, so stop trying to hide from them. In the world's eyes you will never be enough, so **stop letting the world define you.**

Don't let anyone hold you back from your dreams because of your skin color.

You are beautiful. You are precious. You are smart. You are important. You are kind. You are talented. You are significant.

You are Black.

LOVE,
  Older You

THE COLOR PURPLE

BY LYDIA PATTERSON

WRITING IS SUPPOSED TO BE BEAUTIFUL.

Alright, that's a bit of an oversimplification.

Writing is supposed to be a beautifully intricate fabric of words, woven with the sole purpose of making the reader feel like they've come upon some deep, soul-wrenching, philosophical truth that is tugging at the nexus of their heartstrings and brings them one step closer to this ever-fleeting, hyper-idealistic concept of an open-minded, free- thinking meta-human.

And we can't forget the best part. You know, the one where people's imagination takes over? Where people see that the author is Black and decide that the only suitable lens to view the poem through isn't the formalist lens or the psychoanalytic lens or the Marxist lens or the feminist lens because there is only one option and one option only. They read the line from *Season of Migration to the North* that says, "the river reverberates."

It can't possibly be a normal river, they tell themselves. It can't possibly represent the poet's conscience as most archetypal rivers do. No, it's a slavery river–river de Amistad.

African-American authenticity is a lie.

I'm not lazy.
I'm not stupid.
Not angry.
Not bitter.
Inferior
Property
...right?

"If they don't see the happiness at least they'll see the black." [1]
They *always* see the black.
I always see the black.
The world that I describe,
The world that I see - it doesn't matter. All that matters is that
that world is *mine*.

it feels like my soul is stuck
in a bitter, starless realm,
where midnight is eternal
and all peace is overwhelm
by the cold grip of despair
and the pain of deception.
how come my world is shattered
by the sway of perception?

it's this suffocating darkness
that clouds my whole horizon.
it's this never-ending struggle
that's caused my face to wizen—
so i plaster on this mask of steel
to save my fragile heart of ice
so that in the face of hurt and pain
my soul won't pay the price
Let's call this out for what it is:

A distraction.

A dramatic, maddening distraction.

"我愛你," I whispered to Catherine, trying ever so carefully to imitate the rise and fall of her pitch, "我是—"

"Are you part Chinese, Lydia?" Yuan interrupted.

"No?"

I responded, a little taken aback by the question.

"Are you sure?" he repeated, insistently.

"Yeah, why?"

"Well, you can't be this smart and completely Black."

"HEY!" The calling voice forced me out of autopilot. "Lydia!"

I glanced behind me, scanning each of the people in the hallway in attempts to discover the source of these intrusive sound waves. It was Yuan again, and he had that same smile on his face he always had when he was about to say something that he thought was funny. I debated with myself as to whether I should acknowledge his presence verbally or continue minding my own business. It didn't matter, though. I didn't have the time to choose.

"You wanna join the KKK?" He asked, daring to smile.

If one more day had passed since bible study, I think I would have abandoned all morality and slapped that child so silly. "Excuse you?" I snapped.

"You know, the Kool Kids Klub," he responded, grinning even wider "what else would I be talking about?"

'TWAS MY FRESHMAN year in high school. This year, however, was different than most, as it signified a huge transition in my life. No longer was I attending the bougiest public school in Houston - I was attending the bougiest *private* school in Houston. I didn't know what to expect. Before I enrolled, people told me this school had race issues. I didn't believe them, though, because the front page of the website had more Black people than I was used to.

Oops.

I'm not sure how this conversation started—I'm even less sure about how it got *here*:

"I don't even see why you're worried about getting into college," he said in the most matter-of-fact tone I'd heard in a good while, "you have affirmative action."

"What's affirmative action?" I asked, confused. I knew very little about the college admissions process at that point in time. It was news to me that Harvard was an Ivy. I don't think anyone's ever given me a more demeaning look in my life.

"It's when colleges accept people like you... Black people. They need 'diversity' to look good or whatever."

...

What?

...

"You know that's the only reason you're here, right?"

IT FEELS strange complaining about stuff like this.

Not because it doesn't hurt, but because I look back at history and see that my ancestors would've given an arm and a leg for this to be the extent of racism.

Being Black a century ago meant you were subhuman. In the words of the wonderful poet Rudyard Kipling, "half devil, half child." Not even half-*man*.

Being Black not long before that meant you were property. You'd watch as some rabid dog possessed by Satan himself was given more of "Christ's love" by all of these so-called "God-fearing" Americans than you.

Every African-American before my time experienced an active racism that attacked their soul. So, I feel like it would be a slap in every one of their faces to let the mere words of some privileged brat affect me in any way shape or form.

Sentiments aside, I also feel like the fundamental reason why active racism is so bearable nowadays is because it's addressable. Active racists intend to be racist and are blatant and explicit in their actions—and everyone knows it.

Passive racism on the other hand...

There's a convicting sort of touch
in the bitterly scalded hands
of the long-departed shadows
that dance in winter's gelid lands.
They cut excruciating wounds
that scarred my body to the bone...

I FEEL JUST as bad complaining about this too.

I remember that part in *Citizen* when Claudia Rankine analyzed the Serena Williams story. She credited her outbursts to the concept of accumulation. All throughout her tennis career she had been internalizing racism that she couldn't address. Eventually, all of that pent-up resentment came out in an inevitable (and socially unacceptable) explosion.

I want to believe that my situation is similar. That I'm not *weak*. I want to believe that what happened to me was as racist as I felt it was.

... Was it?

THERE WAS LESS than a minute left in this half.

One of us shot on the goal cage. The ball bounced off the goalie's pads, travelled straight towards my stick and I lifted the ball into the goal's net. We all tapped our sticks together in celebration and the buzzer went off not too long after. I jogged off the field, grabbed a quick sip of water, and hustled into the huddle.

"Hey, Haylie, nice goal!"

"Yeah, that was amazing!"

I watched in an astonished silence as half my team congratulated my apparent lookalike for an achievement that had taken place while she was sitting on the bench.

"Wow, Haylie, that was you?" Coach asked.

Did you forget the lineup you just wrote out, Coach?

Someone else quickly interjected, "No-no-no, it was uh, what's her name..." She had her hands on her hips, snapping, seriously trying to remember my name.

A silence fell on the team. In it, I felt an increasing number of eyes shift their gaze to me.

Tap-tap-tap-tap-tap-tap-tap. Tap-tap-tap-tap-tap-tap-tap.

"Haylie!"

Tap-tap-tap-tap-tap-tap-tap. Tap-tap.

"Haylie!" The voice yelled, louder this time.

Tap-tap-tap-tap-tap- Snap. I quickly thrust my stick out in a last-ditch effort to get the ball before it rolled too far out of my reach.

"Haylie [Last Name]!" The voice was near screaming now.

I glanced up real fast. Curiosity had taken over—what was coach hollerin' about now? It didn't take too long to realize that she was yelling at me.

"My name isn't Haylie-"

"You know what I meant."

Did I? Did I really expect the woman who'd been coaching Haylie and I for the past year and a half to mix us up now?

———

Streams of boiling blood run frozen
through the thin pathways of my veins.
Intertwined are the tainted hopes
that seize my spirit with their chains.

I'm suffocated by the wind
and drowning quietly in ice.
How long until my hollow roots
pay a terminal, pyrrhic price.

———

WE WERE PLAYING a small 2v2 scrimmage game at practice. Someone passed a lifted ball to my opponent. It hung in the air, about a meter in front of her. Quickly, I intercepted it, knocking it to the ground, and made a break for the goal.

Or, tried to.

My heart sunk a bit when I saw everyone and I mean everyone leap backwards.

"That was aggressive," she said. The coach agreed. I need to calm down, they said, I'm dangerous.

Minutes later, someone else did the exact same thing.

The exact. Same. Thing.

But, this time, no one leaped backwards, no one even flinched.

"Woah," they said, "that's some good skill there."

From the sideline, I watched in silence as she was congratulated for doing what was considered for me to be a crime.

You're dangerous.

Truer words have never been spoken.

JUST LAST YEAR, I was riding in the van with my club field hockey team to the U16 NITs that morning. They typically fiddled around with the dial until they found a radio station that played suitable music. I tended to lean against the side of the door and blast Christian rap through my headphones.

Today, however, I hadn't brought them with me. Today, they couldn't decide on a station. One of the girls took it upon herself to provide music from her phone. I'd been zoning out, and, in all honesty, I didn't really care for any of the songs they were playing. At least, not until I heard the n-word blasted over the speakers.

"Switch the song," I muttered under my breath.

"What?"

"Switch. The song."

"Why?" someone said in a sorry excuse for an innocent tone.

I was infuriated, and I made sure the glare I gave her portrayed every ounce of that anger.

"Look, it's not that bad," she continued, "they obviously didn't mean it.".

EVER SINCE THAT fateful day at the end of the field hockey preseason of my junior year, when I threw down my racket and said that I'd had enough, I've wanted to scream.

Either I couldn't tell it right, or I just wasn't right. *I can still hear them saying, "You exaggerate."* I'm just a Black teen who's lived in Caucasian suburbia her whole life. *So, tell me, Baldwin, what experience am I supposed to trust?*[2]

What is acceptance? What is *integration?*

It's easy to paint myself to be the victim when I replay these events over and over in my head.

All of them.
Each and every one of them.
Racist.
That's what they are.

That's what the many African-Americans in my life have told me that they are. But I'm not too sure.

That is the core difference between active and passive racism. That is *intent*. When someone intends to hurt you, the enemy - the subject of retribution - is clear. But what about when they don't intend to hurt you?

What about when their innocence constitutes the crime?

CAN I SAY, with absolute certainty, that the discrimination I received from the field hockey community was intentional and racially charged?

Is it fair to me - and the pain I went through as a result - to say that it wasn't?

Who or what is responsible for their response to the upheaval in the universe, brought about by my threatening presence in this white sport, that endangered the broken identity that holds them together?

MY STORY IS STILL BEING WRITTEN as we speak.

I don't know how to end what doesn't have an ending. All I know now is that I have to go
I'm expected on the court.

IMAGINE

BY MAKAYLA TERRELL

Imagine being the only Black girl in class.
Imagine being the only Black girl in honors classes.
Imagine being the only Black girl on sports teams.
Imagine being the only Black girl in gyms at sporting
    events.

Imagine always being asked 'Can I touch your hair?'
Imagine always being asked 'Do you wake up every
    morning and do that?'
Imagine always being asked: 'Look; do you think I am
    darker than you?'
Imagine always being asked are you two related to
    each other because you're both Black

Imagine thinking you were not beautiful
Imagine thinking 'my hair is horrible'
Imagine thinking 'he probably doesn't like me because
    I am a Black girl'

*Imagine thinking about how you were not comfortable
    in your own skin*

Imagine becoming a strong Black queen
Imagine becoming confident in yourself
*Imagine becoming your schools FIRST Black female
    to be senior class president*

Imagine.

*I cannot imagine because this imagination is,
    simply, me.*

COTTON KIN

BY AMINAH ALIU

Black girl:

You must know that America was
the bloody yolk in our eggs,
and the cataracts that prevented us
from seeing the beauty in a lineage long beaten out
    of us.

America has not always been beside us, honey.
Sometimes it has been
over us
Breathing down our exposed collarbones.
under us
Watching us sway from trees
ripe with blossoms.
Sometimes it has herded us like cattle to please the
    masters who needed more flesh
to feed on.

Don't get me wrong, our wombs no longer bare cotton
     kin, but tell me—
How can you love hair that feels so much like the
     plantation?
Why are you still trying so hard to fix the problems
     America forced into you?

You must know that America made problems
as much as it made progress, and that
a knee to the neck is a side effect of
refusing the master's advances.

THRIVE TIP:

Don't wait for someone else to start the conversation.

Open the door and take the first step.
You can do it!

I believe in you!

OLIVIA V.G. CLARKE

D&I ACTIVIST, STUDENT
6 YEARS IN PWI

AFTERWORD

BY TERREECE M. CLARKE

As an author, a journalist and former Black girl in white schools, I am overwhelmed by the kindred spirits of the girls and women in this book. This was the book I needed when I started at a PWI.

These authors, these leaders, put words to those feelings and incidents that are sometimes indescribable. They instruct, reveal - and most importantly - they *heal*.

When Olivia first voiced her idea for the book, I don't think she realized it was a stop-you-in-your-tracks idea. I literally paused in mid-motion. And it wasn't because she is my child... it was because I knew it was a book that was so needed.

This is a book you can come back to again and again. Each time, I find something new. Each time, I am inspired by the writers' courage, grace and vulnerability. Each time, I think, "so many across race, class and gender can learn from this."

The last thing I add is this: Do not pity a Black girl in a white school. SEE her. SUPPORT her. LISTEN to her and BE FAIR to her. Be a consistent support system, good mentors, better friends and a strong ally. Do the work. Don't expect these young women to do the heavy lifting of dismantling white supremacy on their own.

NOTES

The Color Purple

1. Rankine, Claudia. *Citizen: An American Lyric*. London, Penguin Books, 2015.
2. Baldwin, James. "A Letter to My Nephew." *The Progressive*, 1 Dec. 1962, progressive.org/magazine/letter-nephew/. Accessed 16 Dec. 2019.

ABOUT THE EDITOR

Hi, I Am Olivia V. G. Clarke

...a student, leader, and activist in diversity work.

I serve as a leader on my school's Diversity Executive Board, plan diversity conferences and lead student-run faculty development activities.

I'm a proud member of the 2019 & 2020 Black Girls Lead Class created by Black Girls Rock founder Beverly Bond. Additionally, I am a multi-year, full scholarship attendee of the Humanities and Cognitive Sciences Summer Institute at The Ohio State University.

In 2018 I was selected to be a part of the Student Diversity Leadership Conference, a multicultural conference for high school student leaders in diversity. This summer I'm studying Korean as a 2020 Finalist of the NSLI-Y Summer Intensive Program through the United States State Department and making college decisions as a QuestBridge Scholar.

But hey, I'm still a regular 16 year-old senior who has to study for the ACT/SAT and clean my room.

I like to hang out with my friends, dance, binge watch K-Dramas, eat potatoes and listen to all kinds of music. And ducks. I love ducks.

Hit me up on Al Gore's internets:

 facebook.com/blackgirlwhiteschool

twitter.com/oliviavgclarke

instagram.com/oliviavgclarke

ALSO BY OLIVIA V.G. CLARKE

The Black Girl, White School Journal
The Black Girl, White School Ally Journal